IN PURSUIT OF BEING

MICHAEL A. SHAW

IN PURSUIT OF BEING

TABLE OF CONTENTS

FOREWORD

Whilst trying to process and reconstruct his world after the transition of his young mother during his adolescent years, the author embarks on an inward journey that would lead him to re-evaluate his entire existence. Set in the backdrop of urban London in the late 90's, the book details his transition to a newfound understanding of self and 'being'.

This personal account of one's battle to overcome emotional turmoil, provides insightful ways and methods with which we are all able to heal, regain authority over our energetic balance, and realign with our life's purpose post traumatic experience. In Pursuit Of Being is a period snapshot within the life of the then adolescent author and examines the symbiotic relationship between all we desire to become tomorrow, and what we are being today.

1

INTRODUCTION

Although I love the change of the seasons, I have
always had a particular affinity towards the
summer. Probably because I am a summer baby. Thus, it
might puzzle you when I say I was born on a cold sunny
day in March. Allow me to explain. That cold sunny
March Day was the day of my mother's funeral. It was
the first day that clues to the answers I had been so
desperately seeking since her passing, began to surface.

The grief and void were still there, and I felt different. However, somewhere within trying to make sense of all the events and subsequent emotional fallout, etc., she had given birth to my life's quest through her passing. To find out where I am, and who is that looking back at me in the mirror? Hence, odd as it may first sound, and unbeknown to me then, that day was also the day, that unto my realignment I was born!

I am not from a silver spoon background by any stretch of the imagination. Not only were there no silver spoons in my mouth, but I'd also go as far as saying there were none in the entire neighbourhood. It was a densely populated, predominantly working-class area of South London. A zone comprising of a high percentage of single-parent families, most of whom got by due to parents having to work more than one job and social benefits of one form or another. A positive is that humble beginnings can help a person to develop a sense of appreciation early on in life.

Seeing first-hand what effort goes into having just some of the basics or simply having to go without can make the value of things a consideration at the forefront of our consciousness. A reflection that never really left me. By value, I do not mean in a monetary sense. I mean more as in what is 'actually' important.

It was a close-knit community composed of a large contingent of 1st & 2nd generation immigrants from the West Indies, Africa, and Asia. Scattered amongst them were low-income native English & European families. Most families knew each other. Some even knew each other from their country of origin. Aside from the differences in our respective domestic cultural upbringing, the children attended the same schools & youth clubs, etc. We all grew up together. There was a sense within the community that we were all we had. The broader 'macro demographic that existed beyond the boundaries of our estate readily ensured we were always aware of our 'cultural' differences. Still, outside of that, we were all in the same boat.

It was the mid 90's, and we were the inner-city underdogs, dreaming of our great escape in the fast-approaching change of the decade. Those factors serve as a basis and provision for the bond within the community. On this day, all the outpouring of love and support my family had received was not something you could ever buy. I will always be eternally grateful to the neighbourhood angels, who were so giving of themselves in our time of need. Often people fall into the habit of focusing more on what it is they do not have; to the point where they can fail to appreciate what they do. As I looked around, saw all the faces, and absorbed the magnitude of the moment, I knew I was not one of those people.

2

QUESTIONS, QUESTIONS, AND MORE QUESTIONS...

Two questions just circled my entire being like vultures, becoming louder and louder as the stagnant moment seemed to linger and increase in density around me. Where am I? And whose reflection was that coming back at me in the mirror now? Before this day, even though I could acknowledge that I did not know myself, I had thought I had a fair idea at least. That is what added to the daunting nature of my dilemma.

I needed answers or a view of where to start to look to find any. For the first time in my existence, I felt incapacitated. Which way was up? How do I even move, let alone move forward? Which way is even 'forward'? Is it selfishness compelling my tears, when I know that she is now free from all her pain? Should I be rejoicing at her return home? Most babies are crying on their way in, so have we got this entire death concept twisted? Do we even really die? If we are energy beings and energy doesn't die, only transforms, then how is that possible?

My sense of emotional connection to relationships had been rapidly diminishing, keeping pace with my loss of direction. Things had changed beyond my control. Regardless of my lack of readiness to mentally process the eternity of that change, it was what it was. Life as I knew it would be different; all left was me and the unanswered questions. The passing of my beloved Mother was undoubtedly the most impactful and profound experience of my life to date.

Unlike when you are falling physically, it is way less easy to identify when you are doing so mentally. Only in hindsight was I able to see certain aspects of my issues. Grief is something that we all deal with in our unique way. We can often walk around thinking we are ok when we are anything but. In truth, we all like to project to the world that we are strong and can handle anything. Unfortunately, that can cause us to bottle things up and not talk to anybody about how we truly feel inside—simply kicking the can down the road.

The nature of questions is that, like a continuous string, the more you ask, the more there is to ask. Central to any question is 'knowing' when you have arrived at your answer. For example, one usually only feels they have an answer; when they satisfy themselves, they know the answer. What does that say about the importance of 'knowing' something instead of believing something? And at what point do we 'know' something? Is there a clear indication? How can we tell? I decided to mentally scroll through memories of my experiences, trying to recall actions I may have taken, which led me to say afterward, "I knew I shouldn't have done that". It was essential to be honest, as I wanted to see if there was any correlation between any of those moments which I could recall. Some may refer to it as having a 'gut instinct.'

After a while, I soon acknowledged that at those times, I always heard a voice in my head preceding my action. Not a voice in an audible sense of the word, but more in the sense of a resonance, or 'download,' being translated or communicated as such, for its intent of my understanding. What was that voice, and where was it coming from though? In trying to answer that, I explored the relation to it being a 'gut instinct.' The voice was in my head, so what was the gut reference alluding to? I also noted that other than just hearing the silent voice, I also sensed a specific type of energy which accompanied it. Was 'knowing,' therefore, connected to a particular form of source vibration outside of our most regularly acknowledged spectrum of feelings?

Being that so many of the things we do and choices we make are encouraged by emotions, can it be assumed that we can exercise greater control over our feelings through 'knowing' ourselves? I sought to extract the most profound examples from the memories with the most intense emotions attached to them. That was easy. It was the memory of me not wanting to look in my mother's casket at her funeral. I remembered thinking I did not want that to be my lasting visual memory of her and was thus highly apprehensive about doing so.

The voice appeared; however, this time, it was different. This time I had recognised it as being her voice, but purely by the 'energy' of it, as opposed to its actual sonic or sound. Her presence was as familiar to me as was her appearance or how she sounded. The other notable thing was that it told me to 'do' something as if it wanted me to 'know' something. It was telling me to go and look. As I walked up and glanced into the coffin, all at once, I realised that it wasn't my mother at all. That was never who she was.

For the first time, it all made sense, and saw her Earth vessel as 'the avatar'. Up until this point, I had been communicating with the spirit, but via what I thought was her, merely her avatar. It was now time to understand and learn how to converse in another way—one which would be direct with the spirit. The point being all the anxiety I created and had conjured up before doing so, instantaneously dissipated with the 'knowing' that vessel was not her, I 'know' that.

Embarking on this realisation, I noticed that while I had always associated the voice with being one of caution, this was an example of where it was one of liberation. I had always been privy to the concept of universal balance and the duality of such. Knowing something can affect and influence a positive or negative charge to one's emotional state. How efficiently we process what we 'know 'determines how efficiently we can bring ourselves into balance from an energy standpoint. What, though, when we are being indecisive? Could that suggest this was due to blockages inhibiting our ability to hear the voice of 'knowing'? My search for the answer to that question led me to research how we engage with that form of energy. I began to source literature related to the body's energetic centres, the chakras.

During my initial investigation, I would read that although more existed, there were seven main energy centres of the body within various areas. Each centre was like a spinning vortex of energy, each responsible for its specific area of energy management. The seven main ones were the crown, third eye, throat, heart, solar plexus, sacral, and root. I discovered that a blockage in any of these centres directly impacted various aspects of our bodies, in a variety of ways and regions. Not only can it cause emotional imbalances but may also manifest as physical issues. Overall well-being and freedom of energy flow is subject to the optimisation of these centres.

There are corresponding colours assigned to the chakras, reflecting their ultraviolet presence and radiance on an ethereal scale and level. Going back to the voice for a moment though, as mentioned before, it is often referred to as a 'gut' instinct. Could this be due to a high resonance level within that region? Was there then an energy centre located in the gut region? The Sacral chakra is located at the centre of your lower belly; at the back of the body, it would be at the level of the lower vertebrae. Its visual depiction is a deep orange colour swirling vortex. It is the 2nd chakra associated with the emotional body, and its element is water. As a result of this, it is associated with flow and flexibility. It is interesting that when we are in a flow state, we seldom get stuck. As the notorious martial artist Bruce Lee famously stated, "Be like water."

These findings provided a direct connection and answer to the 'gut' question. Still, in accepting that as an explanation for a specific sensation, what of that for the voice within my head? Again, was there a chakra in the region where the voice was seemingly broadcasting from? The crown is the 1st chakra situated at the top of the head. Violet in colour, its key associations are with divine wisdom, unity with all things, that is, our spirit body, and enlightenment. The colour violet is representative of cosmic awareness and consciousness.

This information made perfect sense to me, as although the voice would sound like my own in 99% of these instances, it still felt as though it was filtering through from another part of my 'self.' A part connected to a source, with which I was also energetically linked. I began to understand the importance of keeping these centres well maintained, as not only do they control the flow, but they are also responsible for the consistency of such energy distribution throughout our physical avatar.

Upwards from the 1st chakra (root) to the Crown, the spinal cord acts as an antenna, transporting and directing that flow. When the chakras are clear and in harmonic alignment, our sensory balance is fully functional, and our energetic flow motioning with optimal fluidity. As we know, when we think of things being in harmony, we over-stand that this signifies all within and surrounding us being well. Therefore, our well-being has a symbiotic connection to all we are, being at 'one.'

So, can it be said that being 'at one' is akin to somebody being in perfect energetic alignment with all that is? Something which is attainable through having uncompromised lines of free-flowing energy throughout these meridians, from our root to our crown chakra. The more unrestricted these portals are, the more efficiently they work in relation to one another, providing an enhanced awareness of all things cosmically speaking. Can this chakra be where our higher self-communicates through? It would explain why it would be; this is from where the 'voice' omits...

3

WHERE IS THAT FROM?

When an artist creates a work of art, they have a mental image which they work from to then render as a work of art. At which point, it may be shared or enjoyed by others. It is irrelevant whether that piece of art is manifested as a physical representation, for example, a painting, or, as with musicians, in an audible manner. So, being they can already see or hear it before others can, where is it? It is not visible to the naked eye or the physical ear at the time of conception, so how are they seeing or hearing it? Let's explore the notion that one may be able to share the same vision as another, especially after such a vision is prior verbalised to them. Two heads are notoriously better than one. If we buy into the concept of a higher self, it is reasonable to suggest that it would provide us all with the proverbial two heads.

However, when sharing one's vision verbally, one is simply pointing the other toward the same cosmic space to look, listen or focus one's attention. It's all out there in the ether, waiting to be, heard, acknowledged, and accessed. As the saying goes, there is nothing new under the sun, and everything is everything. As a teacher tutors a student, they point the student toward specific knowledge and where they can locate it. Once the student looks, the insight is there to unfold for him or herself. The process continues and eventually, the student becomes the teacher, and each one teaches one. To my mind, that 'one' is yourself.

Our higher selves can be likened to our 'individual' satellites? Constantly scanning the higher galactic dimensions while filtering information back to us on what it is seeing or hearing, and from which location within the Astral realm, etc. Clarity or ability to receive, translate or access such data with 20/20 vision would depend on the condition of a: our 'antennas' and b: how uncompromised and balanced/ aligned our pathways are.

Within that concept, we can still account for our individuality when you incorporate that we all have free will. This fact would maintain that even whilst observing the same thing from a singular point while occupying the same cosmic space, the potential to have a distinct perspective of it remains. Besides that, with all things being vibrational energy, if the two are not vibrating on the same frequency, for example one may have blockages present in areas where the other does not, that same thing may resonate in a completely unique way, subsequently creating multiple emotional vibrations and thus subsequent versions of it also. We can think of this as we do the concept of parallels.

Let us look at instances where we tell ourselves we knew we should not have done something. For that to be an actual phenomenon would lead us to conclude that the higher self would also exist within an alternate timeline to our physical selves. How else could it forecast a positive or negative outcome of our actions if it did not? We all experience dormant emotions and sometimes trauma from historical events. Of course, we know that physically we exist in the present.

On this line of examination, there appears to be a trinity of timelines in which our two selves may exist: past, present, and future. At this point, let me say no, I am not a meta physicist, or a quantum scientist, and I do not hold any related qualifications from any fancy educational institution and the like which pertain to any of the discussions I bring forth within this book. The topics discussed herein are purely an expression of 'my truth' and a depiction of the journey which led me to it. Is 'on-the-job experience as, or any less valuable than just the theory? Well, let us move along then! I had identified two 'selves' and 'probability' of a trinity of timelines within which both selves occupied and functioned simultaneously. It is a valid assessment that most of us are more aware of the 'present' timeline, and reference past as what we have gone through, and future as that we dream about.

Until that point in my life, I may have settled on that as a comprehension of timeline's and the 'Trinity.' Not on this occasion, though. My recent encounter with mortality pushed me towards a transitional period of accelerated self-discovery. From that moment, all lines of questioning went deeper. The sticking point for me would be the division of time itself. For instance, I wondered why there are 60 minutes in an hour, and whose concept of time was that? An hour is perceived as a much shorter unit of time for a man given a day to live than a young football player who cannot wait to sign his first club deal in 60 minutes is it not. Long before watches, people managed to navigate the optimum times to do things, using the positions of the planets in relation to the Sun or Moon.

I have always been curious about the concept of time travel. As a young boy, I would dream of having a Star Trek Transporter gadget of my own! Maybe it had something to do with the fact that this wasn't something I could just fashion out of old cake tins, as I had my make-shift drums. I would rack my brain trying to figure out how I could also do what Captain Kirk and the others were able to do. Anyway, I thankfully outgrew all of that.

As I matured, I flirted with another theory, which for some reason, just had a stronger resonance within me. Time is a constant, and 'units' of time, as we have come to understand them, are experienced as we 'perceive' them. It is purely a way for us to place a tangible measurement on any given moment dependant on where it is our perception is currently focused.

Have you ever had a daydream interrupted by a person talking to you? Only to emerge from it apologetically claiming you were "miles away?". Well, were you not? Or have you ever had a dream that was so vivid you woke up, and for a few moments, you are disorientated, and it's as though you are re-adjusting to your surroundings? And before you answer, no, intoxicated at the club the night before doesn't count! But seriously, most of us can agree we have experienced these things at some point. That 'real' sense of being somewhere completely different, even at another time, while our physical bodies remained where they were until we returned, to my mind, this can be classified as time travel, more so than the transportation of my physical matter to some other corner of the Universe. So, whilst we are physically within the present, it may also be probable that we are simultaneously in the future and past. Suggesting time travel takes place on a conscious and subconscious level. As it maintained a viable basis for my time as a 'constant' theory, I gravitated to this way of processing it.

I noticed a recurrent theme with words employed to explain a feeling or as a description of an object that also offered a connection. For instance, you may use a spirit level to ensure a picture is evenly lined up when hanging it. It is reminiscent of having a balanced spirit, which requires equal energy distribution, resulting in optimum equilibrium at our centre. In reference to timelines, our perception of ourselves within them would be central to our existence.

On the energetic scale, in the centre is the 3rd chakra, the solar plexus, found at the body's core. It is represented with a yellow colour and is associated with our personality, perception of who we are, and willpower. It made perfect sense to me that this vortex, which is related to who we are, would be within its designated location of the body. This understanding brought things progressively into focus for my assessment. How well-balanced or aligned I was, would directly influence the angle from which I viewed myself. Observing anything from alternate angles will always give us another presentation.

4

DO I KNOW YOU?

There is a school of thought that to learn how something works; you must take it apart. The learning part is in the reconstruction. At that point, life had given me a head start on the taking apart bit, so here I was, figuring out the putting-back-together side of things. Before embarking on this journey, I had not pondered that whenever we pose a question out into the Universe, an answer always comes back. Often a wide and varied selection of solutions, depending on the questions we pose.

We may not like, resonate with, want to face up to, or even believe the answers, but they do if we pay keen attention.

As we exist in a multi-dimensional universe with endless possibilities, being specific about what we desire to know about ourselves offers much aid in providing the answers we seek. Something that I had yet to realise throughout much of the initial stages of my endeavour. I was just so keen to know why I was going through what I was? and if it was down to the way I was? etc. The questions I was asking had a broad spectrum; hence an array of various answers would flood in. They were answers though. Some came via the guise of other situations to learn from or not!

My first attempts at a closer evaluation of myself were too superficial. I was making naive errors of gravitating to that which I did not like about my appearance. This way of analysis, nine times out of 10, is more likely to lead to further insecurities, or feelings of vulnerability. It wasn't until I discovered that finding things to appreciate about who I was, would be beneficial in ways I had not ever prior considered.

There is often much about us that we take for granted. Balance is present throughout the Universe, so if we only knew where to find it, we may be surprised to see the gold in the hills. The parts of who I was that worked in favour of my greater good were the easiest to acknowledge. All it took was identifying what I felt most comfortable revealing to others. However, the realisation that disowning the other parts of myself would never change the fact that it was still me was a big step towards personal progress.

They were a part of me also. It was all me. Loving only the parts of me I viewed in a good light meant that I would never indeed be able to love myself as a whole unless I acknowledged the rest. Otherwise, I would only deny myself the love I felt I deserved or should get from another. Alternatively, If I could love all of myself, I would always have love, regardless of whether I was in a relationship with a significant other. It would not matter.

I never wanted to assign anybody the task of bringing out the best in me, and I always saw that as something I was responsible for. The best of me is what I wanted to be able to share. That was even more reason to address all aspects of myself. Not to say, I needed to be perfect, saintly, or anything like, meaning that even at my worst, I could always represent myself with the best version of myself. Getting to a space where I could face all parts of my being objectively without judgement was paramount. Doing so would provide me with a foundation. It would also lend assistance relating to areas requiring appropriate healing. Bringing forth more accomplished internal peace, as such, was the quest for self-mastery.

The intricacies and complexities of who we are mean that our evolution of 'self' is an ongoing journey. Often one which requires us to be 'thick skinned'. Paramount when avoiding any excuses we make for ourselves, to swerve confronting those aspects within us, that are long due for an overhaul.

I was not from a religious family per se. Most of my elders had more of a spiritual persuasion than a religious one. A degree of subtle tact was always employed when handing down valuable lessons. The dots were always there to be connected as you grew into your maturation. For instance, if my mother or grandmother were not as keen on my choice of girlfriend as I was, in sparing my naivety, they would not just say they did not like her without a valid reason. Instead, they would wait for an opportune moment to remind me in passing, "Don't watch the body. The body will change!". In other words, what is inside a person is what really matters, not to put too fine a point on it!

The thing with life lessons is some can at first seem like a riddle and take a while to decipher. Once you get it, though, they stay with you for life, as do all universal truths. As I became more familiar with the painstaking process of peeling back the layers, it became easier to accept what was there to be revealed instead of just pretending it was not there. Not that it was all bad, just that no problem gets solved if not first acknowledged as one. To see ourselves for who we genuinely are takes courage. It is also a pilgrimage that brings us face to face with our shadow side. Merely scanning the surfaces will never cut it. There is much knowledge gained from our light and shade alike.

Before going through an experience, we may think, or at times may like to think, that we know how we would cope with or handle a particular scenario should it arise. I was finding out you can and may surprise yourself. Who gets a 'life, and how to get through it' handbook at birth? We live and learn. And for as long as we live, there are always new aspects to us that we discover. As with modern technologies, our application of what we learn determines enhancement, or detriment to ourselves, our experiences, and our ambitions.

Regardless of how I felt about it, I had asked questions, and answers came back in various forms. It was like being thrown into scenario after scenario. I wanted to discover who I was, and the Universe intended to show me. What better way than to allow me to learn from my experiences? I later understood that the Universe does not tell us who we are. More so, it observes who we are and conspires to provide the things we ask it to. The familiar 'Be careful what you ask for' saying has a wise sentiment behind it. What shapes our experiences in the 'present' directly correlates to the nature of the energies we interface with, known as our thoughts.

We often describe our mood with words that constantly remind us of the bandwidths in which these energies reside. For example, when experiencing feelings of depression, it is commonly referred to as feeling down or low. On the contrary, when we feel good, it is said that we are on a high, elated, or in good spirits. The high/low references are like a barometer for the level of frequency we are vibrating at. Low being dense, and high being light and accessible. Emotions consistent with low-level frequency are fear and anxiety, whereas the higher levels are associated with joy and bliss. If you imagine a transistor radio, you cannot receive access to FM transmissions on AM radio, as certain stations only exist within specific bandwidths.

As with Universal frequencies, the principal functions in the same way. The higher we can raise our vibration the more bliss we can access within the regions they are present. The higher the frequency, the greater the quality of the signals we can receive from the quantum field through a more coherent reception with reduced interference. Some utilise conduits such as crystals to help harness specific frequencies they are said to omit and transmit.

For reasons I did not know, I was always naturally attracted to crystals more than jewellery as an accessory. It had always felt they held secrets of other dimensions within them. From an early age, I had often been told by one source or another that everything is connected. However, initially, I could not relate to how that was possible. I mean, there were people with whom our vibe just did not mix. It was not until some way into my re-education and increasing evolution of awareness that the concept began translating to me.

My conclusion is that all that we are, namely mind, body, and spirit, has access to multiple parallel dimensions. All that exists does so in a number of these realms all operating in adjacent motion, everywhere, all at once. For the voice in our head to have the ability to pre-warn us, prior knowledge of the outcome would have to be possible.

Many of us go through various relationships throughout our lives without having an actual relationship with ourselves first. It is something few of us understand, know how to do, or grasp the importance of. As with the Universal laws, it is not something which we are actively taught. Not liking or being able to spend extended periods alone can sometimes indicate one's buried issues with themselves. Being alone by choice removes the distractions we can sometimes cling to in avoidance of facing the shadow self. The 'fomo' phenomenon highlights the extent to which this is prevalent.

More often, we would sooner do anything, for fear of missing out on something, than spend that time alone. Can you miss out on something more significant than expanding your relationship with yourself? I am not suggesting that one cannot have a fun time with others, enjoy a night out, etc. But if, for whatever reason, you were unable to make it to the show that night with your friends, is it really that serious? So much so to attach 'fear' of missing it? I suggest not and argue that the more time one can give to oneself, the more harmonious and able one is to accept what one sees within themself without the need to attach any amount of disappointment to it.

In general, if all is well within yourself, one can say all is well in their physical & spiritual worlds, the two work in tandem. It provides us with a good if I make it, good if I don't scenario, leaving us less affected either way. We have all met a person that is one way at the start of a relationship, and by the end, they are not who we thought they were. We can only draw such conclusions from getting to know them, right? The relationship with yourself works in the same way.

As with all our most successful unions, the more nurtured, the more satisfying, rewarding, and fruitful they are. Just as an attentive partner knows how to calm their partners anxiety, or lift their mood, a person who knows them-self, knows how to suppress their ego. The knowledge and understanding of self can also be beneficial to others with whom we share our lives. With this knowledge, we can pick better suitors for instance, and align with that which aids in serving our greater good. If it were our first non-family related relationship, post-romantic encounters would have an increased percentage chance of working out. It is harder to lure someone who knows who they are into a situation when they know it is not for them.

A good relationship with the 'self' is also paramount when aiming to manifest anything in life. The more comprehension you have of something, the better positioned you are to be able to utilise its full potential. If you know who you are, then you know what you want. The more aware and in tune with that understanding, the more specific you can be about what that is. It all bodes well, as the stronger and more focused the intention will be towards its attainment.

How good does it feel when we buy something for ourselves that we 'really' want? Or something as basic as treating ourselves to a massage?... We can all relate to those heightened feelings we get of satisfaction when doing for 'self.' Being a 'self-made' anything is also often attached to a higher level of independence. Whenever I am alone, I remind myself that some quality 'me' time has never hurt anyone.

5

IS ANY OF THIS REAL...?

How we deem what is 'real' varies from individual to individual. We derive our beliefs of what is 'real' primarily from our perceptions. However, we are all liable to change our perspectives or perceptions at some point, are we not? So subsequently, can we alter what is real? Well, if we consider that the definition of 'real' is (*existing as a thing or occurring, not imagined, or supposed*), I may argue no.

How much of what seems 'real' to us, is 'real' in its true sense? Since the mind is susceptible to entering an array of altered states, identifying our state of mind is vital to gaining overall control of our being. As previously mentioned, blockages within our energy centres can create a warped sense of reality. I struggled with this occasionally whilst coming to terms with grief. Not knowing how to cope with the situation initially, I gave my thoughts free rein to figure out a way.

The problem is, when left to its own devices, the mind can often play tricks on us! While I did not lose mine, making sense of all the white noise it was spewing out was a complete task. Before long, I saw that an unsettled mind would never serve me long-term. What I needed was a rational one. At this time, I began to practice stillness, attempting to slow everything down in my head, afford myself space, and bypass at least some of the myriad of emotions. It was whilst utilising this method that I began to see; it was my lack of acceptance of what 'was,' causing a lot of my issues throughout this period. I was constantly wrestling with something which I could not alter. It was a no-win battle. What had happened and I had experienced was real, and what is real is real. There is no change or substitute for that. Understanding the importance of acceptance was another pivotal point in being genuine with 'myself'

We are encouraged to understand and engage in the 'appropriate' ways to best interact with others. How best to interact with the parts of us which are not visible is something that is overlooked. I wanted to be able to condition myself to identify precisely why a particular thing would historically trigger a reaction within me. To begin to do so, I would employ a mental count of 10 before saying or doing the first thing that came to mind. To a greater extent, this inner interaction assisted in suppressing responses born out of ego. I am not going to say that there has been a full departure of the fire that burns within, but it did reduce my desire to meet any vibration outside myself with equal or stronger polarity. Going from 1-100 took it a little longer!

Through this discipline, I began to realise that I was only responsible for my actions and not that of others. There was no need or requirement to adopt or take on the energy of anything external, which I did not wish to. I started to see how easy it was to de-escalate a scenario by just consciously deciding to, based on what I deemed to be true to myself. Whatever someone's opinion of me was, it was their opinion. Regardless of what that may be, they were at liberty to hold whatever views they wanted. Did it mean that was who I was? Of course not. It is always within our right to consciously agree to differ and move on without further argument. It is I alone that can affirm 'I' Am in reference to me.

For those familiar with the concept that we exist within a matrix, you may allude to all projections around us as being pure illusions. Whether that be the constructs of the societies we operate within or the information we are mass fed for a 'wider' social control, etc. We are bombarded with data which often dictates who we should be, as opposed to that which encourages us to attain our most authentic divine purpose.

We are born innocent, and many beliefs get programmed through intricate indoctrination methods. When we begin to re-code this programming, we can start to see and re-establish who we are and only give credence to an accurate summation. It is common for people to feel as though they cannot live without another, or do without a physical object, etc. Well, unless we are talking about the sun, water, air, or food, as 'real' as it may feel to them, it is nothing more than the effects of a compromised emotional state. With the equation for manifestation being mind over matter, when illusions penetrate and manipulate our thoughts, they quickly confuse our perceptions and shape outward reality beyond our desire.

There are many differing views on life after death. Whatever your stance on this matter, I have yet to see anybody leave this physical realm and their material possessions, including their body, go with them. For those who believe in an afterlife in whatever form, it is always the spirit said to be immortal and that which goes on. To me, the higher self is the most significant part of our makeup. It only deals with what is true and that which is 'real.' The fact that it doesn't need anything from the physical world to exist speaks volumes about the legitimacy of our perceived physical realities.

Our senses are like a circuit board through which we can interact physically within a seamless virtual reality setting. However, is something less real because we cannot touch or see it? Can we see carbon dioxide? Once able to embrace being more open to what is outside of what we are programmed to accept as being true, we become more adept at bringing ourselves closer to our full potential, surpassing self-induced limitations of tainted belief systems. As I see it, we are spirit beings having a partially physical human experience. We are the amalgamation of full-spectrum vibrational light source energy.

The totality of our existence extends beyond the bounds of this dimension. The seats of the combined higher and lower self-dictates we are multidimensional beings. My personal inclination is in support of the concept that the expansive possibilities within our very design are a testament to the magnificence of the source of our primary conception. No other creation of this world compares to that of the human overall. The technology within us contains as higher potential of any known planetary life form.

Such is how powerful we are that we can conjure up realities for ourselves without any element of truth to its foundation just by buying into the illusions and visualisation; However, the rampant ego, left unchecked, can seldom be relied upon to provide a solid foundation for self-honesty, let alone reality. It is even more reason why maintaining a fundamental relationship with one's higher self is essential. 'real' is a by-product of truth; hence, where 'truth' is found, you find what is real...

6

WHAT DO I WANT...?

On the surface of it, the question 'What is it that we want'? should be a straightforward one to answer. I found that it was always anything but. When asked, my brain would scramble to produce relevant answers. To be honest, I would say that most of the time, I would probably respond with references to meaningless material objects. In posing the question to others, I discovered it goes for most of those I asked. I wondered if this was because we often associate success with excess. People often view ownership of material objects as a way of self-validation. If we are to look to things outside of ourselves to validate us, what when those things fade away or are no longer there?

No one product, possession, or item of clothing in existence, should or could ever say more about who we are than we do. An expensively wrapped gift does not automatically speak to the value of the gift itself. It is a given that there are infinite possibilities, so narrowing our 'wants' down to just a few things can be tricky, dependant on how we compute it. There are no right or wrong answers. It is wise to be mindful of what we profess we want and how it serves our greater good. I pondered on whether what I had thought I wanted was in any way coming from the point of selfishness or somehow trying to fill in any voids I may have felt were present in my life. As far as that was concerned, my one redeeming quality was that I have always had tremendous empathy toward others.

During a conversation with a crystal healer, I was asked what it was I wanted. After my first three answers, there was zero acknowledgment! I tried to think of something more substantial, but my mind was blank. The fourth answer I gave was greeted with a sigh, and the reply, "Do you even know what that is"? It was not said in a way that insinuates that I was stupid but more as an encouragement to dive deeper. It was also a call to remain aware that not everything is as it appears to us. Hmm..slightly 'awks', but I received the memo, and promptly stopped throwing out random answers!

I knew I needed to apply more consideration before I could articulate what I was searching for. I left the conversation that day but continued consciously recycling my answers in my head repeatedly for the rest of that week. I placed them all in a mental box, where I could look at each objectively to see what it was about those things. Also, could they correspond with each other in some way? What did they represent to me exactly, or indeed say about me, or the way I viewed my life and the things in it?

As time passed, I became more aware that what I was trying to articulate was things I believed would, on some level, give me a sense of contentment. My given answers were constructs of my inner programs, which I may have unconsciously felt offered some degree of security, or used as a form of self-validation. I realised it was not about any of the things I had mentioned. I wanted to be content in my life, with who I was, how I was living my life, conducting my relationships..., and just at peace in all areas. That was it concisely. There was also something else that I knew I always wanted that would also facilitate both my quest for purpose and contentment. Finding a way to do something that benefited as many people as possible was always up there on my bucket list. No amount of external material possessions delivers any of those things though, and certainly not for any real longevity. It is common to see billionaires who cannot realistically spend what they have in a lifetime, still have an insatiable desire to want more. Remember that one item you always wanted that, if you had, would make your world a perfect place? Only for the novelty to wear off several months later, you needed the next latest item. It is a compulsive reflex.

There is always an affiliation between inner peace and contentment. When no internal conflicts are present within us, we are more readily satisfied and for a more sustained duration also. We do not lean so much towards filling our world with things to compensate for unresolved emotions or energy blockages. A more harmonious state of being is realised. Subsequently, everything external to us becomes secondary to what lies within. At times, people may want something just because they see somebody else have it. In this instance, the motive is stemming from jealousy. The expression 'keeping up with the Joneses' springs to mind and encapsulates the behavioural pattern.

The notion that one must be somehow better or out-do the other, is unfortunately a common one in the world we live in today. Once we allow the wider society to dictate who we need to be, we are susceptible to losing touch with our own uniqueness. Internal communication breaks down, and engagement with a synthetic form of consciousness ensues. When we are not honest in our assessment of whatever it may be that we want, in comparison to what it is we truly need, what most may spend their lives accumulating, serves in no truly profitable way when seeking to achieve ascension.

I had arrived at a place where I had started to grasp the concept of being more selective with 'wanting.' As I did, it unveiled another perspective. It is said that the Universe conspires to present us with what we put out. If what we keep putting out there is that we 'want' things, it gets interpreted as if we are requesting to be in a state of 'wanting' something instead of realising it. There may be a missing link in the chain of manifesting and attaining what we desire. For example, outside of things of a physical nature, when our 'want' is to be a particular thing, is it enough to 'just' want that? On further examination of this theory, I realised that you could only 'become' something by prior 'being' it.

Instead of rehearsing for the part, we should be assuming the role. You cannot be a doctor before 'becoming' a doctor. The entire process of studying, passing the exams, etc., is a path of the course of the 'becoming' conclusion. Ever heard that you 'got to be' in it to win it? On an even more basic level, a nice person is so, simply because they are 'being' nice. Should that alter, they are then 'being' something else. People who have self-healed after a significant injury or illness commonly talk of visualising themselves 'being' healed. We are clear that the body is designed to heal itself, but seeing itself as 'being' well, was relaying to the Universe what it was they were to 'be.' It led to them 'being' healed in the physical sense. What if the 'being' part of us, as human beings, is a long-forgotten knowledge and comprehension of our divine blueprint?

Does just 'being', open the gateway to experiencing that which we allow our free will to? Imagine, we could extract the 'wanting' to be anything and just 'be' that. From there, as long as we remain on a consistent path, the journey and necessary energy exchanges, leads to our becoming. There is much to gain from bending oneself instead of attempting to bend the spoon! With this theory, contentment was back in my hands. All I had to do was to have an appreciation of my life and all its experiences. In addition, be thankful and content while remaining open to receiving. A half-full glass not only comfortably leaves room for more but also contains 50% more than an empty one.

If at times we can alter our perspective, we can begin to see that there are always reasons to be grateful for something. Even our greatest master teachers may appear in the form of our greatest adversaries. Some may serve as the challenge we need to overcome, to advance through our soul missions and spiritual pathways. Indeed, from time to time, it is quite probable that an Ike Turner, may be the catalyst which propels a Tina Turner to a whole next level of greatness.

7

WHAT WOULD I CHANGE...?

I often considered, if I could view my life to date as a movie, what would I change if I could? Would it be my lines, my actions, my global standing? Everything? As tempting as it may be to make some adjustments here or there, there is no way to calculate the actual effect of making even the most minor change. You see, I have arrived at the point of authoring this book as a direct result of all that I have gone through or experienced. Different circumstances could have easily configured me differently, leading me to subscribe to the illusions of a material world. What does not kill you can lead to you rebuilding yourself to be stronger than before.

Thankfully, I am alive at the point of writing my first book to give gratitude for what I have learned. The culmination of my experiences has afforded me a degree of personal expansion. I can recognise that every person, every event, and every situation, has played its part in the narrative of my story. Whether favourable or adverse, there have been lessons in both equally. As an example, I may have stayed in a relationship longer than I should have. But nobody ever had a gun to my head for me to do so. It could have just run its course. Just simply arrived at the point where both parties learned lessons they were supposed to. Thus, it served its actual purpose. As a way of understanding, that takes the prospect of being a victim off the table and presents an empowering benefit from the eventual outcome.

We blossom and emerge into maturity, and our individual purpose is present within all eventualities. Therefore, as I see it, nothing happens before its time, even if, on the surface, it may appear the contrary. In some cases, 'success' is attained exceedingly early on in life before there is the required level of mental adeptness to deal with it. In those instances, it is common to see that followed by a cascade of lessons that need to be learned for that individual to transcend the incoming scenarios and subsequently growth occurs.

Often the ones who come through that maturation experience stand as accomplished individuals. We never stop learning, but it is how much truth is there to what we gather that gets us to the point of expansion. For some, when they talk about them 'doing this' and 'doing that,' it is all about the future. They will view changing aspects of their past, as an opportunity to alter the outcome of their current 'present.'

I am in constant expansion because of the discoveries made from the process. At times reconnecting with parts of myself has been like having the most cleansing of detox. That is not to say every experience has come with an overwhelming ease to face up to, but I am certainly better for it after the fact. It is like a person coming off a drug; for all the pain caused, the benefits far outweigh the difficulties faced during the transition All of us, indeed, have forms of suppressed memories that may lay dormant within us. Should they go unprocessed, they have the potential to manifest themselves unsuspectingly.

These manifestations can often show up as physical ailments within our bodies. Constructive observation of ourselves allows us to process better what we may otherwise sweep under the rug instead of resolving. We are formed of galactic light. Cells in our bodies can hold and store data throughout our entire lifetimes. Once triggered, that information seeks a way to be released.

There are other considerations to just going back and changing aspects of one's life. Being that everything is interlinked, should that be done, it would have a domino effect on all the other lives I have shared or co-existed with. Nothing is in isolation. With every action, by consequence, there is a reaction. How even a single change may potentially impact the life of another is something that there would be no way of knowing. At an earlier stage of my life, I could have produced over 100 things I would change via the chance of a 'do-over. However, today, I have learned to focus on changing that which can be and accepting that which cannot. Developing a comprehension of knowing the difference can make huge differences to the quality of one's mental health.

The point of any such adjustment should only place me in a better situation in the now anyway. Which I can say I am, regardless. Observing and acknowledging the unsavoury aspects is an asset-rich exercise. The issues come with holding on to them. There is also a difference between us passing judgement on ourselves as opposed to just observing. When we can be entirely forgiving towards ourselves, we can bring forth re-'soul'-utions, and heal, without having to send anybody else's lives into an uncertain trajectory!

8

PURPOSE

For many, the purpose question is not readily considered until confronted with a feeling of being lost or having experienced a loss of a loved one. Of course, I had entered this category myself. My purpose for doing or wanting to achieve anything was solely to provide a better life for my mother. That was it. I had watched how hard she had to work and her struggles throughout her life, and I wanted to give her everything. Once she had transitioned, I did not know what anything I was doing was all for anymore. What does it matter now? The one person in the world whom I had wanted to make proud of me was no longer here to share or enjoy any success I may have with me. I wanted to give back so much and show my appreciation for everything. I was completely shell-shocked. I was still young at the time and had not gotten to do all I had wanted to for her, which at that time, made me feel as though I had failed. I had to find a way in which to regain my motivation.

I became more conscious of my mortality during the period directly after my loss. I was not particularly bothered about dying at all; it was more about what I was living for. I was feeling empty, disorientated, and disillusioned with purpose. A deal I was working on at the time, had finally started to come to life, all at the same time the life I was doing it for, was transitioning out. As irony would have it, I ended up closing that deal, however my first major purchase was to be her tombstone.

What is the reason that I am even here? I wanted to understand what the purpose of living a life was all about. It was a distinctly trying time for me emotionally. The following 8 months would also bring with it the transitions of my grandmother and grandfather. The word drained does not come close to describing my energetic state at that time.

Whilst trying to figure it all out, I gradually began to see that any divine task I could have would really be about me. For example, my purpose had always been about my mother, but I never had absolute authority over those circumstances or outcomes. For all I know, my mother could have fulfilled her soul's mission and thus left this dimension on doing so. If what I had always considered was my 'divine' purpose, fulfilment of it could never be possible once she had left. I became aware that whatever preordained assignment I may have in life can only end at the time of my passing. Which suggested it had to be something that would span the entirety of my journey here. My take on 'purpose' began to take on a different shape.

Time and circumstances permitting, I could have given my mother the most without achieving a higher level of vibration or personal ascension. I saw how I had been confusing purpose with a sense of desire. No matter how noble a gesture, it was never as I had originally thought. Had I been able to deliver on all I wanted to, once having done so, would I then be in a position of no longer having any other purpose? This revelation was a new awakening for me; I was being prompted to evaluate my existence in a new way.

The term 'born to do it' is often touted when someone excels in a particular area. Our egos readily buy into this, and we can follow a path or belief that reflects that narrative. For instance, the fact that we may be great at playing football does not necessarily mean that our purpose in life is to play football. There may be many things that a person is great at, so how accurately can we determine our purpose if we use that as an indicator?

Sometimes, possessing a particular gift or talent is purely a reliable tool through which we can configure certain aspects of our lives. How we can best utilise and share them in a way that is impactful to others is the thing. I have been able to travel the world due to an ability. Along the way, I was also fortunate enough to make a living deploying my skill. As it came so naturally to me, I had just assumed it was something everyone could do and had initially taken it for granted. I never considered the reason I was able to do it or if it had any connection to any ultimate divine purpose I may have.

It was not until many years later I became aware that what I could do, has always been central to any personal transitions throughout my life. It was providing way more than being able to travel or make money. It provided a pathway to all I endeavoured to do. It was my vehicle that transported me from point A: to point B: Whether it was why I met certain people, got to see parts of the world, had specific opportunities, relationships, etc. Across the board, its impact was present in all areas of my life.

Although I had various attributes, this one was the 'go-to,' always integral in bringing about any new direction. Once utilised correctly, it could even ultimately deliver actualisation of my purpose. Something that I only recognised through my newly embarked upon practice of meditation. It dawned on me that via all the opportunities my ability brought me, it had also presented opportunities to others. In some circumstances, in terms of opportunity, even providing a voice to others when they felt they did not have one.

I had to become disciplined to where I could cast aside the voice of my ego. The stillness was what I had found best enabled me to do so. I had to step away from being moved to do anything, or make any decisions, based on any self-indulgent echoes. The ego seldom shows us what we need to be aware or appreciative of. Often, it is a voice of 'suggestion' which leads us to think we can do anything. However, doing anything is not necessarily doing that, which leads to attainment of our greater mission. I do not personally think our purpose is to be found through suggestions. Today, I see it as our true purpose being a thing we reconnect with. The re-understanding that we are all accountable for what the experience of this dimension can or will be.

We are all in coexistence, so there is no getting around that. How we choose to do so is determined by our own decisions. Reconnecting with a divine' purpose' is something that once we do, we 'know' and recognise. It goes way beyond that which is a random feeling or presented as an audible mind generated suggestion. It is a clear directive, that projects within the soul with such clarity, that when we eventually land on it, it is as apparent as night and day. Within the range of my capabilities, what I loved to do, and what I aspired to do outside of benefiting just myself, was where I rediscovered mine.

There are many different views on what happens when we do not fulfil our soul's intention. One of the most common is that we may return to the Earth plane to do so. There may be no way of knowing for certain whilst we are still physically represented in this plane. It is fair to agree though, that the feeling, we experience from completing anything is one of satisfaction. It elevates our spirits from within, even after completing our most minor endeavours. The implications of such gratification for the soul throughout a lifetime are monumental and enable us to spiritually ascend into the higher dimensions. It raises our essence.

As with a video game, once you complete the tasks of each level, your reward is a move on to the next. Is that just art imitating life? Looking at the lives of certain individuals of prominence, who over the historical course of their existence, it appeared, had landed on their predestined objective. I observed that their calling impacted their lives and, at the same time, the lives of many others. It was as if; their purpose also gave back. With all things being part of the whole, our divine calling would also be impactful to others.

For examples, Malcolm X and Muhammad Ali left behind iconic legacies that defined their lives and who they were. They were transformed individuals by the end rather than at their stories' conception. The transformational aspect of their being was always edging them closer to their realisation of their purpose. Such was the nature and strength of their soul contracts, that not even the bullets that were intended to kill them, could succeed in doing so. Their legacies live on, inspiring generations long after their physical passing. Any attempts to silence them, only ended up immortalising them on t-shirts! The spirit of who they are lives on and is still felt within their words left behind.

On the other side, there are also those who (it may be deemed) have had a more negative impact on the world. It does not mean the point of their being was anything less relevant though. It could be that their purpose enabled the world to observe where we are, regarding our ascension as a collective, hence highlighting the importance of their existence. It is also why I would suggest that it is who we have become by the end of our stories that is key, as that is what lives on.

To me, this is what the journey of life is about. Unfortunately, so much emphasis is placed on money to 'make a living.' No amount of money can make you live forever in a physical sense. It is the soul which is immortal. I wondered in what ways it may galvanise and serve us if we remained present to the notion that whatever we were 'being' directly impacts what the overall global collective experience becomes.

9

THERE ARE LEVELS TO THIS

The concepts discussed throughout this book are based on a condensed version of my journey. It is my individual take on what I have learned or experienced over the years. I started at a low point when I was looking for more. The search has continued to this day, as we never stop learning. Things did not always fall into place or where I perceived the area in which they should fall. Neither did they necessarily translate to me straight away either, but that's where acceptance also plays a significant part in seeing beyond that.

Sometimes, my comprehension of the theory of certain things took a while. Typically, the sheer levels of programming we endure mean that a total rewiring of our understanding is required to see some things as tangible. For most of the time, we exist in our own microbubbles and seldom consider the bigger picture, let alone see one. Questioning what part our lives play in the greater ecosystem of the Universe is something other than what may sit at the top of our agendas.

It is said that knowledge is power. Within every moment, there is an opportunity to take another step towards spiritual empowerment of the soul and edge closer to reclaiming our energetic sovereignty. Albeit, that step is heading in the right direction, of course.

At the very least, remaining open to exploring and researching the less talked about topics relating to our existence, allows us to extend and expand the potential repertoire of our being. Hence, we become better equipped to apply 'useful' consideration to those steps we proceed to take. Inevitably with life comes challenges. A question for consideration is, does darkness not reveal unto us where the light is?

I have found that applying principles, which I have learned, has afforded me context over challenges, and a degree of clarity on the best way to navigate them, for my greater good. Of course, beyond the subconscious mind, no one person knows everything. Collectively, as a race of beings, there is much that we must learn. We can employ disciplined practices into our lives to render the development of our highest form. The more coherent and connected we become to our source of creation, the more information we become exposed to from a higher divinity to help us to achieve our desires.

Everything is in constant perpetual motion, and we are all at various levels of our spiritual development at any given time. In no aspect does this make one better than the next. Learning from each other would be problematic if it were different. Our oscillation amplifies when surrounding ourselves with those of like mind or frequency. On the other hand, there is also much we can learn from those who are not. We rely on each other in ways that are only occasionally obvious to us. The bottom line is the journey must start somewhere. How fast we move along the path is dependent on us.

A plan commonly precedes travel. We recognise when we arrive simply because we know the location of our desired destination. Thus, the importance of us knowing that information speaks for itself. The next part is figuring out how we are to get there or what effort it takes to do so. Our curiosity as to how, can be stimulated in many ways. It may even be on a subconscious level, whereby a decision we make unknowingly leads us on a path we had no idea could take us to our designated destination. It is like the moments when something just worked out the way it did. Although you may like to take the credit, you cannot accredit it to one particular action you took. The optimal route is not always one which is evident to us. Now and then, we end up on the back roads, and it appears we have lost our way. Just the right turn, though, and we are back on the main road.

I hold my hand up to the fact that historically, I have been a serial overthinker. Before deciding on certain things, it was common for me to endure sleepless nights, exploring the many potential outcomes. That was more born out of wanting to make the 'right' decision instead of being overall indecisive. Not only did I have to learn the 'process,' I had to learn to trust in the 'process' also. The two would naturally go hand in hand, right? But no. I was learning new ways of viewing and receiving data, which I had no iron-clad physical proof of. Much was down to how it was absorbed and reverberated within. You know when something strikes a chord with you.

Thoughts of whether I saw certain things incorrectly, or was leaning towards this aspect, or that because of ego constantly crossed my mind.

At first, I had not even realised that I was already in the beginning stages of the process, as I was still caught up emotionally with self-pity. I wanted a change of fortune, and I wanted to see it right away. At that point, I was looking for an instant return on any investment of belief. It is about an energy trade though. The universal laws work how they work, regardless of whether you believe in them or not. Once I understood that, I humbled myself to accept the process as all-encompassing and that it would be what it would be and take as long as it took. There are no shortcuts or cheat codes involved!

Accepting this one detail paved the way for me to mindfully become more open. I could just focus on learning without placing any unobtainable expectation on myself to reach enlightenment by any self-designated point. Like anything, to improve, I had to strive to do things in ways that were more empowering and complimentary to my elevation and do so consistently. That was all I needed to retain a consciousness of.

10

MIND YOUR LANGUAGE!

I am sure that at one point or another in our lives, we have all heard the saying, "be careful what you ask for, as you just may get it!". Well, it is certainly not without reason. Taking accountability for one's actions is an area of our self-dialogue, which I had to pay keen attention to. Even in informal communication with others, our use of language is a crucial factor. It directly affects the eventuality of any desired outcome. The semantics of words are as powerful as they are potent. In fact, neurolinguistic programming is facilitated via usage of words and visual stimulation.

On closer examination of my word choices, it became more apparent why we refer to the formulation of our words as '*spelling*'! I began to see how words were literally our external commands to the Universe. Without us being mindful, we can quickly and naively impact the turnout of such instructions. For example, we are often encouraged to chase our dreams. However, 'chasing' something would indicate it is moving away from us.

It is also common to hear people talk about 'making money.' Can it not be suggested that if you need to make something, either you do not have it, or do not have enough of it, hence require more? Would it not be more powerful, & more to our favour, to say that we are getting money? Or that we realise our dreams? It is, without any doubt, that love is the highest vibrational frequency. Therefore, I questioned why we should look to 'fall' in love. We would enjoy more significant gains from elevating in love, no? Yet still, songs about falling in love have historically been the biggest-selling songs year after year. That said, speaking as an awarded songwriter, today's mainstream offerings may, let us say, be on the path of alternate bounds in its oscillation!

Are we not subconsciously setting ourselves up for failure? Or constantly being encouraged to use language which, on the surface, may seem optimistic but are merely inverted negative affirmations? To provide some context, many may judge me as miserable if I classify happiness as overrated. That is understandable, given the relentless programming for us to identify happiness as a defining goal for ourselves from our conception. However, happiness is nothing more than a subjective and fleeting emotional state. One can easily be happy one minute and depressed a few hours later.

I was starting to comprehend that to be joyous in life speaks more to one becoming bountiful on a far grander scale of emotional consistency. I, therefore, maintain to be in joy throughout my life. Unfortunately, most of us have gone through our lives unknowingly casting 'spells' on ourselves and each other.

A few definitions of the noun '*spell*' state the following;

- A form of words used as a magical charm or incantation: A '*spell*' is laid on the door to prevent entry.
- A state of enchantment caused by a magic '*spell*'
- A magician may cast a spell on himself.

- An ability to control or influence people
- Had magical power over them: he woke from her *'spell'*.

By no means are our thoughts any less impactful. When I reflected on just a few points in my life, I started being able to see where I had thought myself out of a situation. Alternatively, where I had thought myself into a few! Often it is referred to as having to 'get out of one's head' or our 'mind playing tricks on us' Thoughts become things, and everything first starts with a thought or a vision on the meta-physical plane.

It took time to accomplish mindfulness of staying present. With so many sliding doors, smoke screens & illusions at the 3D level of consciousness, it's an ongoing mastery. As is said, a thousand-mile journey starts with the first step! With the Universe being as old as it is, our knowledge of it is clearly still in its infancy. As we move through the ages, it becomes increasingly evident that we have only been interacting with but a fraction of our innate abilities. The inception of inverted concepts of reality, has long been an enemy of our true state of inner sovereignty.

In order to complete a 360-degree whole, energy travels 180 degrees in one direction of its polarity, before being met by 180 degrees of its opposite. The integrity of balance is maintained in this way. Highlighting the same amount of energy that we put into a negative or low vibrational thought is the required amount for a positive one. Since an energy transfer is required when manifesting anything, there is always a needed alignment to the assignment. I made it a point to stay awakened to this, as it reminds that we always have a choice of polarity with which to rendezvous. As previously established, both can bring outcomes on opposite ends of the spectrum. Operating from zero point of contradiction means I could experience evolution while existing in this paradigm of duality and quantum soup.

When thirsty, I became appreciative of my glass being half full and less concerned that I could drink double what was in it. There is appreciation within gratitude, which is why we all like to feel appreciated. If, as is said, everything is everything, then we can never really be without anything. Hence, can always find something to maintain a humble disposition for. Again, I choose thoughts and feelings of gratitude & joy.

Life is always on the move. A variety of situations are constantly coming and going. How can we then best affirm and define what it is to come towards us? Nothing in this dimension, which is of a physical nature lasts forever, so the sooner we come to terms with that as being a fact, the easier it becomes to accept the going part. If we want an Uber, we order an Uber. At a restaurant or takeout, we place our order. In both examples, we are expecting a desired outcome. When we 'order' anything, we expect it to come to us as we have set out, do we not? It is because we understand the power attached to 'ordering' something. As we do this, we give a specific and direct vision of what we desire to attain.

As with a computer, the command key sends instructions for executing the task. This is an order being sent. Engaging with language as a set of 'commands' when seeking to manifest effectively can be a potent means of actualising the desired outcome. Given that we are co-creators of our realities, what are we 'asking' for? Should we not just be creating? We will create a scenario for ourselves, whether conscious of that fact or not because we all think and ponder regardless. Language empowers, destroys, elevates, or suppresses; it covers the entire gamut. Either way, like our thoughts it will create an outcome for us, one way or another. How we choose to use it best is solely up to us.

11

AND NOW FOR MY NEXT TRICK....

Ok..., so I was making progress, slowly but surely. The demolition site, which was my emotional state, was starting to take on an appearance more in line with a construction one. I was contemplating things which I had not done before and pursuing a path of higher learning. As with any healing process, to do so, we need first to realise the need to do so, which means acknowledging and facing up to the problem. For me, that time was now.

As young children, we develop much of our behaviour patterns from those in our immediate vicinity, whether family, friends, communities, carers, etc. We absorb and adopt many of our views and stance from our environments. Most of the time, we are oblivious to the actual reasoning behind many of what we assume to be 'our' beliefs. Numerous scientific studies address the correlation of generational traumatic DNA. This is a form of trauma passed on via our ancestors or even via the womb. This being the case, what percentage of who we claim that we are, are we really? How much of the baggage that we carry belongs totally to us alone?

I wanted to let go of all of what was not mine and rid myself of the heaviness of having to be or live up to the expectations of others. The more I 'unpacked', the more space became available, eliminating mind clutter. It allowed me to see that everything was simply perceptions and projections. Being able to differentiate between them accurately starts with being honest with oneself. When we are not, we open ourselves up for others to project their perceptions of us onto us.

Our true power comes from within, not externally. It is from within that all is created and subsequently released. It is why leading a horse to water does not guarantee it will drink. It was, therefore, up to me to define who I was and stand on that. I understood this. In addition, I also started to grasp the essential nature of learning to accept others for who they were. That way, I could begin sorting through the bags that did not belong to me! Not all of us who may feel we are overweight are so in a literal sense only.

Evidence that a shift was occurring within my self-awareness began to appear. I started to see how my transitioning affected others and their subsequent interactions with me. It became more noticeable how people often want us to be what they want us to be. Primarily, people engage with us for who they perceive that we are, as opposed to who we are as a person. I had heard that we attract 'like' energy and witnessed that formulation within some of my relationships with others.

We all realise our evolution at different rates throughout our lives. How many times are we told, "oh you've changed"? In my case, that was encouraging, as change for the better was what I was looking to do, in the development of awareness at least. Those who understood and could accept me as I was in the now were whom my journey could continue with. All outside of that had served their purpose in my story as an overall experience. Either way, it was neither a good nor a bad thing. It just is what it is. It was not for me to judge others, although we are all observers at the end of the day. For me, I was always more bothered about being understood as opposed to being liked. Others not agreeing with something I thought was never a huge issue. All that mattered was that, at the very least, they knew what I was and what I was trying to say. We can always agree to disagree without placing each other in boxes.

Growing up in the type of environments that I had done, caused me to be what some may refer to as, a little rough around the edges! If asked, I say what I think. For some, that may come across as abrasive. Some may even label it as being complicated. As impressive and extraordinary a creation as we are, are we not all complicated in one way or another? Had I been a 'yes' person, that may have made me less complex and more 'simple' in the eyes of those who computed things that way. My truth was, life had not been easy or 'simple' for me though; what can I say!? However, in the sense that for anything to be universal it would be a requirement for it to indeed be simple for benefits of a wider probability of understanding, I would say I view things in an uncomplicated way.

Considering that we celebrate people throughout all industries for having an 'edge', the complex narrative could seem contradictory. Whatever though, I knew I would never look down on my upbringing or see it as anything less than an enthralling experience. It had galvanised me in ways that nothing else could have. If that meant there was a less tamed side to my character, then hey, I was not mad at it. As long as I maintained my integrity and did not allow myself to be compromised, I was ok with that. Steadfast within this mindset would serve with beginning to start to love the person I would subsequently present to the world as 'me.' I have never been a 'follower.' I AM that I AM. Mic drop!!

12

G.I.G.O! (PRONOUNCED AS GUY GO)

Some of the best memories of my life thus far are from my school days. It was such an eventful, colourful, and fun-filled period of my life. Every demographic of race, culture & religious belief was present at the establishments which I attended. I engaged with them all. Aside from all the mischief we got up to, one memory has always remained at the forefront of my mind. Odd as it may seem, a computer teacher said it in my first computer studies class. Weird one, huh! Mr. Spiers was a computer professor who adorned the appearance of your stereotypical bearded genius. As if he was a direct descendant of Einstein or knew everything there was to know! Anyway, with all he had taught, I always specifically remembered that the first rule of computing was 'garbage in, garbage out.' Displayed on the screen, clear as a Caribbean day G.I.G.O!

That statement resonates today, as it was a quintessential universal truth. Not only applicable to computers but indeed to life itself. It is a fact that computers are replicative of the technology and functionality existent within our divine designs. As it stands, the lack of actual spiritual development within our so-called 'modern' societies can be partially attributed to our insatiable consumption, & inundation of the G.I.G.O factor. So much so that sadly in recent times, we have seen a considerable rise in people going to extreme lengths to get the garbage out! As a disclaimer, when I say 'spiritual,' I am not referring to religion, or anything of a religious nature.

The more energetically, sensitive, and mindful I became, the more I could determine the frequency of any information or vibration I was in the presence of. Various information will resonate with us in other ways for a reason. Even the sources mattered. As my consumption of information had risen exponentially, it was essential for me to simultaneously retain a level of discernment. How the detail resonated with me was equally important, if not more, than the data in black and white. The pen is mightier than the sword.

Words become things and thus influence us and our ability to access or create all we affirm for ourselves. I would only fuse with a percentage of what I consumed as information. I found that there are nuggets of things that I did, scattered throughout the mountains, which I did not. It became about learning what & why something struck that inner chord and how it 'felt' in terms of its resonance once it had. I approached all incoming information with an open mind. If I had all the answers, there would be no further requirement to look for any would there.

Looking back, at the time, I had taken for granted the expansive nature of cultural diversity to which I was fortunate enough to be exposed. People were just people and accepted on their own merit. You liked someone, or you did not. It was never about their ethnicity or background. That stuff was more so for disgruntled adults or the odd kid who had already come from a home filled with intense prejudice. For everyone else, the programming had not fully gotten its claws into us at that stage. It may explain why we develop much faster when we are younger. We are more inclined to mingle with a variety of social groups. The exchange of ideologies is thus more prevalent.

We are learning and growing, but we are doing so together, which is something to note as we coexist. As a species, the advancement born out of togetherness is unrivalled—common customs precipitate culture. Demographic separation can often breed miscommunication, disinformation, and misunderstandings. Not the best scenario for effectively building flourishing and cohesive communities on a micro or macro level. A greater understanding of our differences provides a broader overview of who we all truly are, period, both historically and presently. We are then more adequately equipped to place context and perspective that we are not necessarily privy to from within our immediate circles. The greater the level of our proper understanding, the greater our ability to see the garbage for what it is and not succumb to its stench.

13

NO QUICK FIX

Throughout my life, I have witnessed many associates struggle with depression, due to a sense of lacking. In many cases, drugs of various kinds, whether prescribed or otherwise, were employed to provide short-term refuge. I saw first-hand how this would only paper over the cracks but not address the root of the problem. The closer I drew to the source of mine, the more empathy I had for those struggling to face up to the basis of theirs. It is by no means an easy thing to do. Looking at one's inner reflection can be challenging, let alone staying the course to digest that image fully.

Taking responsibility for issues much easier to pass off than those of others takes a great deal of humility and being brutally honest. None of us are perfect, nor should it be about trying to be so. I know that I'm definitely not! That is an unobtainable reality, so I was not looking to become that. Neither am I expecting perfection in anybody else, but just trying to accept people for who they are and trust them to be who they are. If I can do so, it becomes harder to experience disappointment in others or myself.

There is always more that we can learn, and once we know better, it becomes up to us to improve and do better. I just wanted to do better and become the best version of myself. There were, and to this day even, challenges at every step. The process is one of constant unravelling. It is one thing accessing knowledge and then a whole other consistently implementing it. The lessons and realisations are only able to benefit us by their application.

Along the way, I would fall back into negative thought processes, bad habits, etc., but at least I began to have a reference point I could realign to. That was positive, as without seeing the fork in the road, how would I discern which side of it I was walking on. The journey is one of exploration and discovery, swings, and roundabouts. Getting over the hurdles would take conviction, patience, and a considerable degree of humility. At times I felt as though I was in a tunnel. Just a never-ending dark empty tunnel, wondering if I had gone the wrong direction within it, as it appeared to be so long.

I encountered someone who had said something to me at a certain point, which helped my resolve. They imposed upon me the fact that a tree takes as long as it takes to grow. We may see an adult Redwood and amaze at the sheer scope of it without considering it was once a bud. I started to give credence to what something 'will or could become' more so than just viewing it as the completed article. There is no hey presto moment with the process, whereby you just get the entirety of everything all at once. Although saying that, at each stage, it became more apparent that the changes were actually taking place within the spaces, between one step and another. Things get created within every instant; it was just about how I observed it all.

On many occasions, I had to remind myself that energy must first go through a metaphysical process before forming into physical matter and showing up within our physical realities; it is transmutation in its entirety. Having a lack of patience with ourselves, or how we may judge our development, only means that such transformation will not be thorough, let alone sustainable. We must nurture seeds and prune our flowers for them to grow and flourish. However, if we are the ones planting those seeds, we do not need to wait for them to grow before we know what they will eventually grow into. Should we allow others to plant those seeds, then there is no telling what it is that they have sown or what they will develop into.

As much as we may put things out there, we should also be aware there is much we can extract. In a world where many of us are so concerned with validation via that which we claim to own, we are liable to forget that not even our ideas are necessarily ours. They are all in the ether. We are tapping into what is already there and available to all for download. The level of our vibrational frequency determines what information we can access, but it's all there. I am sure we have all experienced having that great idea that we did not move on, only to witness somebody else come out with the same idea. Simply making vision boards consuming copious amounts of literature on universal law and getting hyped doesn't cut it. As previously stated, there must always be an energy exchange to cause the visualisations we hold as dreams to form.

There is always a requirement for action to accompany the thought. It is always about giving to be able to take, cause, and effect. I like to think of it as the two 'C's'; we call things into our realities and catch our thoughts! So, I would give my time and enlist focused passion towards my cause to no end. I decided there'd be no waiting for my flowers to be given to me; I'd grow them!

Speaking of which, many within the conscious communities allude to us being 'star seeds. To my understanding we plant seeds for them to grow. So, what are our seeds, and where do they grow? Well, we can say that our children are our seeds. However, the land bears more than one type of fruit does it not? So as by way of my recall, I would say to you that the Universe is our land, and our beings are seeds which are planted into it. With that said, aside from apples and oranges, what fruit would you say it is that our world is being adorned with? The phrase *the fruits of our labour* starts to take on a different connotation. Conscious thought is hardwired to reflect the cosmic principles keeping in line with laws of attraction.

14

WHO IS ALL OF THIS FOR ANYWAY?

My process and experiences are reminiscent of a baby learning to walk. I did not just start to grasp all the information I was gathering straight away. At times I questioned, what am I doing all of this for anyway? It was frustrating and often uncomfortable. It was not going to bring my mother back either. I was not going to be able to make her proud of me as I had always envisaged that I would one day do. So, what for? Those hurdles are high and hard to leap in moments. I had to have something with which to anchor to. So that I would not get dragged back into my grief, I would draw on the hardships I saw her go through to provide a better existence for myself and my siblings. Her love, efforts, instilled discipline, and strength would not be in vain on account of me.

She had not just seen something in me; she had felt it. As a child, I had overheard her reiterate this to an uncle of mine. I had no idea what it was and did not understand the statement then. She had not been able to articulate to him what exactly either, just a feeling. There was my anchor. I would, at all costs, find out what that feeling was by exploring who I was to no end. She said it in this kid is different, but in a good way kind of vibe. I was not her first child, so I knew it was not down to her being an excited first-time mother. My desire to understand the meaning behind the statement and its context was always a trigger to get back on track. It was not like an ego thing; I had just always been intrigued as to her meaning.

As I grew older, defining differences started to surface. These intricacies were primarily to do with how I analysed things, or may interpret them compared to many of my immediate peers. Or the cross-section of the demographic I hung out with at varying times. Nothing was ever really a 'set' thing with me. On the surface, it could quickly appear to an on-looker as if I were indecisive or had no sense of direction in life. The truth is, I did not! Things unfolded for the most part. It was as if each stage of life was a mini life within itself. Each section differed from the next, with new cast members, configurations, settings, and energies with which I interacted. Employing overview made me see that throughout the various stages.

I never morphed into a product of any one environment. I always remained the same individual, just becoming more expansive. I had only considered that once I began my quest. Could what my mother had sensed be that I would remain my authentic self regardless of whatever situations I stumbled into or whatever company I may keep? Maybe she found comfort in that. It never appeared that she was overly concerned about me getting into waters above my head, or perhaps she had just sensed a 'freer' spirit within me, which I had no idea may have been the case. I was not doing anything intentionally or recognised that in any way as a 10 yr old! It is also likely any real concern would have been my apparent wandering along nature. A mother always wants to know that her children will find their way in the world, right?

To this day, I meet people from my youth, and the common theme is for a remark comparing my physical appearance in relation to what they recalled it being. On that surface basis, to most, I have not changed much. But so much has, within me, so much has. My wars were fought internally though. Any previous scars were emotional and not visible from the outside. I never came across as overly confident whenever I did not genuinely feel that way, so any obvious changes in my outward display of confidence, was nothing that would really stick out.

Inner and outer projections of us are often vastly different from each other. The people we are in private seldom reflect who we pretend to be in our public lives. Put that down to peer pressure or insecurity. We often create false images of ourselves, seeing it as a way of protecting ourselves. But what is perpetuating this constant feeling of fear within us? What are we so afraid of? Usually, it is the unknown or failure. Or that we have forgotten who it is; we are within the context of our creation and all the innate power that comes with that. What will they think about me if? What if I am not accepted? Liked or even attacked? Well, what if we just be who we are and stand within our power. That is also a thing right?

Encapsulated within our thoughts are infusions of our state of mind. Fear comes in all forms, lack of self-worth, hatred, jealousy, etc. Usually, these thoughts are a tapestry of our past experiences. Dwelling within the fear vibration for any length of time, before long makes us perceive ourselves as being inferior on a variety of levels. Soon, an inferiority complex is developed. Aside from doing so for the explicit purpose of healing, the more we reference past traumas, the more susceptible we are to being trapped within them. Not to say that self-reflection is not a beneficial thing to do occasionally. What we need to be cautious of is a constant dwelling on the emotions of our pasts. Instead, only use it as a reference to assist in navigating our way forward. This practice transmutes any that may lay dormant or have been catalogued, only to be used for rationalising why things are so bad for us in the present.

Our paths are our 'personal' paths, and any positive changes within myself that I could make at a micro level were great. At a macro level though, the journey, and my experiences, were always one for us all. One which we could all, in fact, share in, tap into, learn from, access, relate to, debate, or use in some enhancing way.

It is a given that we all experience growth in a biological sense. But we are more than our physical bodies. That is just one aspect of who it is we are. As multidimensional beings, it is also uplifting to explore how we can grow the spiritual aspects of ourselves. The unique balance provided in doing so brings us closer to being 'whole' as a totality of our creation. The whole is the sum of the parts, the collective consciousness. Whether we see ourselves as being 'spiritual' or not, we function outside that which is purely physical.

There are always distractions, which sometimes keep us glued to this 3D reality. Unable to perceive what may exist beyond it, let alone benefit from it. But it is not by way of the physical form, in which we are all connected, that is clear. If we can engage with that as a concept for a moment, the bigger picture comes into focus. However big or small a part we believe we play in this life is irrelevant. Each role contributes in one way or another, adding a unique cosmic data point to the experience we refer to as 'life' on Earth. Hence, what we do, is for either the greater vibration of all or vice versa.

15

THAT'S HOW YOU SEE IT

For all I was doing concerning my shadow work, many seemed more concerned with that which I was not! I noticed how we could often be preoccupied, more so with what is not happening than what is. Or what something is not, instead of looking at what it was. I wondered if that was because we had become more attuned to feelings of 'lacking' than gratitude or appreciation. Counterproductive, for sure, when seeking to manifest higher levels of existence for us. Gratitude places us directly on the path of receiving. If we are not content with ourselves, how liable are we to find contentment within others? We would always be finding faults. Somebody or something will always be 'lacking.' in some way. Sometimes people who are not content with their achievements inevitably begrudge others of theirs. Or get some perverse gratification in pulling you down in an attempt not to feel so bad about themselves.

Remarks get made all the time, accompanied by "don't take it personally", not understanding the comment more than often speaks to who 'they' are. You see, the more conscious minded I grew, the more the mere vibration of others spoke volumes to me. I had read that there was a time when our communication was done telepathically. As some have grown less aware of their spirit aspect, they have become less aware of what it was communicating about them.

The feelings of 'lack' can often be one of many wounds to the spirit. When this happens, we begin to operate from a defensive stance—feeling the need to be protective of these metaphysical wounds. As it is said, hurt people, hurt people. That being as it may, lest we contemplate what a hurt world does to us all.

On the other hand, we are considerably more content with others when we feel they agree with us. So then, it is something that we are possibly 'lacking' ourselves, as that would suggest, a need to seek something external to our being to manufacture validity of our' emotional state. That scenario indicates we are out of engagement with our true power. Again, if two heads are better than one, then there must remain 'potential' gain in another opinion at times. Staying objective and open-minded, is often highly beneficial to us. But it is paramount that one goes internally to best align with that which is their authentic self. You cannot please or be all things to all people. It is just not feasible. But who ever said that you had to? The aim is to 'be' to 'become' all you are. It is our own light which we should first seek to project, and not that of another. Neither must we allow or solely rely on others to cast our light for us. What if they decided to switch it off?

We often prop our egos up on others singing our praises. And should the singing stop or the song change, the insatiable ego attacks the self. The dance is over, and the light goes out. To 'our' hearts' content, we must first seek to sing our song and dance our moves, and to our own rhythm. When we are in that space of bliss within, we can see its effect on those around us. It makes us attractive to others from an energetic standpoint.

Those existing within this space, are often the ones we refer to as being the life of the party. Speaking from a holistic substance free viewpoint!

Although I became more informed with regards to 'my' being, I was not concerned about converting others into 'being' like me. Others not agreeing with the way I viewed things was not something that I found overwhelming. I understood that they were at liberty to hold their own opinions. If we all agreed on everything, what was there to learn from each other? Outside of the subconscious, no one individual knows it all.

We are each a fractal of a greater galactic conception and as individually different as our fingerprints. We neither set the exams nor grade them, on any higher position, beyond our egos. Convincing ourselves that anybody is doing something right or wrong is, usually down to our own delusions of grandeur. I mean, right or wrong for who precisely?, as according to whom? I would be more irritated that the way I felt was not something people would consider than any disagreement of that itself. It is a reason I align with the doctrine of all things being energy related.

I started to replace right or wrong sentiments with the terminology low or high-level vibrations. The frequency resonates within me on one level or the other. Being greater, lesser, or equal to. There were no hard feelings either way on my part. So, it should be vice versa. We are all just trying to figure this experience out in one way or another. Observation need not go hand in hand with passing judgement. Sometimes, a thing just 'is.' What may be considered as 'normal' to one, may be the polar opposite to another. It remains imperative to stay grounded in that understanding.

Each has their own mastery and uniqueness. Respect for this fact facilitates our harmonic integration throughout our conscious incarnation. Besides, in a world of infinite possibility, what and who holds authority on what defines normality? And why would you want to be regarded to as 'normal' when there is so much more you can be. Shine your light! The blatant fact is that we are individually all different at the micro level, so the fascination of not embracing that, seems bizarre when we really look at it that way. Offer zero apologies for being different, as that is how we are created. In truth, everybody having the same two phones, computers, or wearing the same clothing etc, is far more of an abnormality. Something to consider maybe.

The deeper I went internally, the further I started to zoom out of the external 3D hologram. I began to feel detached from things that I had previously allowed to affect my outer worldly constructions. The grief of my experience had dumped everything on top of me all at once. It was as though I was sitting in the front row at the cinema so close that it blurred my vision. Up until this moment seeing beyond my pain had become impossible. But once I had reached the tipping point, I could expand my outlook, and it was like the lights gradually turning on. Revelations and downloads were pouring in. With my newly attained oversight, I was like, wow, what on Earth are we all doing? Seriously, as a global collective, where are we heading and what are we achieving? Was this the absolute best we could do? Or just the best we can do at this stage of our development. Can we seriously rejoice at what we have done to, or created, as a place to call our home?

Things we place so much value on, like cars, jewellery, and material possessions, have zero intrinsic value at all to warrant levels of our attachment to them. There are millions of material objects that we obsess about. We place more importance on these things than we do on nature, harmony, or even each other. If we all want joy in our lives, how come most of what we have created is material?

Indeed, it would make more sense to generate more joy instead. It dawned on me so many of us were walking around out of focus. If we are still determining where it is that we are or are going, how are we to be able to arrive there? The best position to see the entirety of anything is from a distance. Stepping away from things enhances our ability to do so. Thus, the further we go internally, the less acclimated we become to the illusions of the external reality.

16

IN THE LAB...

In general, I was making some progress. The journey I had begun had, in many ways, channelled my focus. It was not as if the hurt or the pain had magically vanished, but it was no longer the only thing occupying my thoughts. I was beginning to emotionally 'feel' more, though, in a separate way. The numbness started to subside. It was as if my senses were coming back online. Along with the original ones, a few new ones also.

It is funny how, at certain random times in our lives, something said to us previously that confused us suddenly makes sense. Our comprehension of it kicks in. At these times, we can see the beauty of the connecting dots. That moment of enlightenment communicates something we have always previously overlooked. When it happens, it often reveals what was right in our faces the entire time. It allows us to see that we can choose how we look at things. A choice that we seldom even consider. I have experienced many of those moments along the path. There is one, though, that after all of this time, and all I had processed, has only just happened.

Throughout my youth, I was very much into sports. I was always very athletic and loved to compete. I enjoyed challenging myself in that way. The bragging rights that came with the win were just all part of the fun. The cherry on top. If I am honest, I must admit that as a fan, I am a terrible supporter of professional teams. When it came down to it, I did not care that much who won in a game in which my chosen team was playing. I just wanted to see a great match/game played at an elevated level. If an opposing team had a superstar playing, I would like to see them show out regardless. My friends did not quite see it that way; neither did the other supporters at the games!! But I mean, why wouldn't you want to see that?

However, when playing for any of my teams, which I did, or in any single or doubles sports, let's not get it twisted, it was all about the 'W'! Make no mistake about that. We wanted to win, and we wanted to look good doing so too. Unlike some of my teammates who would get super emotional about the whole thing, I just liked the challenge and of course, those bragging rights.

I remember my basketball coach with much regard. May he RIP. He was an amazing man, full of wisdom. In hindsight, we would eventually learn so much from him, gems of life wisdom that went beyond the confines of sport. He would tell us that no matter what happened, he could live with the outcome if we gave it everything. More importantly, as a life lesson, we could always live with ourselves. He'd let us know that if we did that, we could always walk out of the gym with our heads held high. He would only really go off if he felt we had not given everything. Just a very motivational man overall. But yes, that was totally wasted on us at the time! We were like, we don't know what coach is going on about, but we are not about the losing vibe! That is not what we were in the gym to do—or what we bought our new Jordan sneakers for! You do not so readily buy into that philosophy when you are in a group that snubs the "it's the taking part..." narrative. The way we saw it was we could just as easily be taking part in a date right now! No, if we were there sweating and doing all this exhausting training, come game time, we want to win. That's what's good. Besides, the winners got the hottest dates! Which was right up there with the rest of the accolades.

It was not really until I was authoring this book that I reminisced about an interaction I had with him in my youth. We had lost a game. A few of us had gone around to his house that night to hang out. I remember him being surprisingly calm. I was not expecting that. He was a very, very animated coach at the games. He talked with us about the game and outlined why we had lost. We did not have a fantastic game, but we played hard. As I was leaving, he saw me out. "What do you think you could've done better tonight," he asked. Nervously I replied, "Well, being that we lost, probably everything." "We did play hard though." He looked at me and said, "The way to turn your loss into a victory next time out, is to learn from it." "That doesn't just go for sport, it's with everything." "Sometimes you gain more from being on the losing side, than you do being on the winning one." "It's what you do coming off the back of a loss that determines if you recover and come back stronger or not."

As I sit with the concluding chapter of this book, I notice that it is the anniversary of my mother's passing. It seems uncanny that this statement should be one of those profound enlightenment moments. It provides another depth of vision. I had restricted myself to the loss aspect of the bereavement experience, which only compounded the emotional struggles. I hadn't even contemplated that there was any potential victory that could even be a possibility. But in context, he said that the opportunity to learn comes with a loss. That is a gain is it not?

You can return stronger from experiences you reflect on by holding that intent in mind. I see now that I had always been looking at and experiencing only one aspect of the situation. I had never approached it with the sense of balance which exists throughout all things. All aspects of our universe are about balance, regardless of whether we see it at the time or not. We are all subject to the governing laws of being in harmony or not, internally, or externally, across all aspects of our lives. The cycle of our transitions is no exception to that.

On this day, I now understand and have learned how to go forward and celebrate a life instead of mourning one. Life is a wondrous gift to be celebrated. I embarked on my journey, aiming to feel and be better on arrival. Today through my process and the pursuit of being so, I am thankful to know

I have become so. If I may ask you to consider..., what is it that you are 'being' today, and how will it best assist you in 'becoming' all you desire to 'be' going into your tomorrow?

17

(I THINK I GOT IT, MUM)

At 16 years of age, a beautiful young girl from the Caribbean travelled across seas, to start her new life on European shores. On arrival, outside of her family and family friends that had arrived before her, she knew nobody. At age 49, she made her transition from the 'physical' reality. At the time of doing so, there was not an available seat in the church at her send-off; many were standing. That was a testament to how many lives this young woman had in some way impacted within her brief time. She was survived by three children. As a single parent, she raised them with love, morals, and discipline to serve them throughout their lives as they grew up in her absence.

Bearing witness, I had a front row view of her trials and tribulations. Battling and overcoming obstacles, her strength, resilience, and determination were nothing short of amazing. She was a warrior of divine standing. The definition of divine feminine energy. Earlier, I told you of a time when she referred to me as being 'different'. I also told you that it had not been something, that she had been able to further articulate in any definitive way. As I write these words today though, I recognise that I was a child whom she would go on to give birth to twice, once in this physical realm and again from beyond it. In the aftermath of her transition, I have found new life, and thus the rebirth of myself, unveiling the elusive gain from experience. That was possibly the real difference her higher intuition-had communicated to her. Regardless, I will be forever grateful and love her eternally and unconditionally. This book is written in honour of, and dedicated to the expansiveness of spirit which is my mother.

18

CLOSE

In closing, I thank you for your time and wish you well with all your pursuits. May unconditionally love and peace be ever present with you. To my forever soul family, I love and am grateful to you all. I am truly thankful for all your love throughout this Earth experience we have shared together.

To note, indeed there are many courses of action one can undertake to address the issues around the topics of discussion. For example, talking to a therapist for sure has its benefits and assists with the emotional unpacking and refiling of potential problematic memories we tend to hold on to. What makes self-help such a powerful method, is the fact that all change is activated within the self. We should keep in mind that the moment directly after we are impacted by such trauma, is the moment that we are moving away from it, and on the road to our recovery.

As said, things happen within the spaces, one moment can look vastly different to another. It is ahead where our future is situated, and therefore where it is we should focus our aspiration and attention. Whatever it is we are looking at, appears to us as it does, depending on where we are positioned. That is why it is important we establish our own points of view. Negatively charged memories are best utilised for the purposes of navigating our way ahead, as opposed to constantly reliving them, and allowing them to be dictating our present.

We co-exist, so are never really alone. However, as stated earlier, conversations with self establishes a stronger understanding of, and a closer union with ourselves. With this comes clarity, which is basis for actualising exactly that which we forecast for our future accomplishments.